200 Tricky Spellings in Cartoons

Visual Mnemonics for Everyone

Lidia Stanton

CONTENTS

ACKNOWLEDGEMENTS

Thank you to all my students, past and present, for their tremendous enthusiasm for mnemonics. Massive thanks go to my son Harry for sharing his boundless graphic illustration expertise.

1 WHAT ARE MNEMONICS

Mnemonics are memory triggers that help us remember things we easily forget, for example tricky spellings. We can readily recall mnemonics because of their funny and unusual associations with things that are part of our daily lives. Best of all, mnemonics require almost no effort to learn.

The word 'mnemonic' is pronounced with a silent front letter *m* [ni'monic].

2 HOW TO USE THIS BOOK

Look up the word that you find difficult to spell – each chapter lists words alphabetically.

Reference books like this one don't need to be read from cover to cover.

Enjoy the cartoons with visual hints and story lines. They are designed to be funny, silly, bold, and occasionally cheeky (a bra is mentioned three times).

Okay, some story lines are plain bonkers to make them more memorable. If you want to learn to spell in a fun, intelligent and virtually effortless way, open up your mind and let your imagination run loose.

Think of the story behind each spelling mnemonic. Make sure you understand the connection. Don't be discouraged if some hints make more sense than others.

Own the story – modify it so that it makes full sense to you. Think of your past experiences and link the spelling to your own stories.

Use the newly learned mnemonic the same day. We tend to forget most of what we learn within the first 24 hours.

The best way to learn is to teach. Share the spelling hint with other people, in person or online. Tell them why it works for you. Show it off in the classroom, in the office, or use it as a party trick.

Be practical. Create posters and other artwork with the spelling hints and display them around your home to remind you what you've learned. Make the artwork as fun and colourful as possible.

Turn the cartoons in this book into colouring pages. They've been left black and white so you can use highlighters and colouring pens to make your learning active and fun. Be creative. Own the cartoons.

3 CONFUSING PAIRS OF WORDS

These are words that sound the same but are spelled differently (homophones),

or

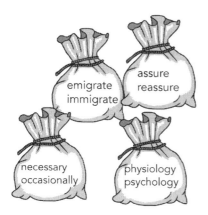

words that somehow 'go together' – either because they belong to the same word category, or because they have similar meaning or spelling patterns.

ACCEPT vs. EXCEPT

ACCEPT

A-C grades is what colleges will <u>accept</u> for course applications. See the smug face on Annie Cinnamon's face? She's been <u>accepted</u> on an <u>ac</u>ting course.

Colleges a<u>cc</u>ept <u>c</u>redit <u>c</u>ard (<u>cc</u>) payments. But if you're 16-18 years old, you don't have to pay. Yay!

EXCEPT

Okay, so you know the names of the boys in a famous band created on the X-Factor except for the fourth one.

I can help you here. His name is… Uhmm… I forgot.

My memory is good except for really important stuff.

ADAPT vs. ADOPT

ADAPT

All living things have evolved to <u>adapt</u> to <u>change</u>. Every day we <u>adapt</u> to fit in.

It fascinates me how Adam's green tracksuit is the exact colour of the shrubs behind the running track. In fact, I'm struggling to spot him right now. I don't think he likes sports very much…

ADOPT

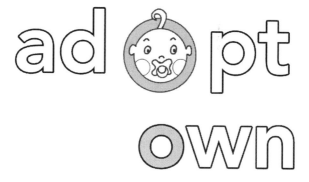

When you <u>adopt</u> a child, you <u>own</u> them and they <u>own</u> you, for life.

Ask an <u>adoptive</u> family if they remember a time when the child didn't live with them.

AFFECT vs. EFFECT

AFFECT

Amber's stunning looks <u>affected</u> Freddie's ability to see where he was going.

EFFECT

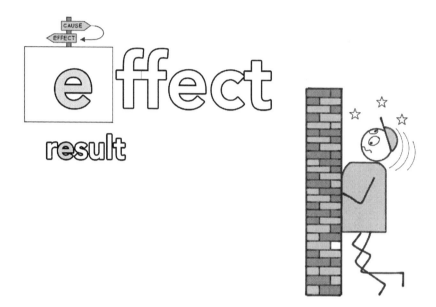

The <u>effect</u> was less stunning.

One person's <u>action</u> (Amber applied a new lipstick that day) <u>affected</u> the behaviour of the other.

And the <u>result</u>, or <u>effect</u>?
Freddie is love-struck. Or is that a 'wall-struck' <u>effect</u>?

ASSURE vs. REASSURE

ASSURE

Ashley <u>assured</u> Mr and Mrs Pleasant that he was the best neighbour they could wish for: "Rest <u>assured</u> I don't play loud music and I'm not into partying. You won't get any trouble from me. <u>Sure as</u> a pickle."

When you <u>assure</u> someone, you tell them with confidence that something will or will not happen, and they usually believe you.

REASSURE

Sadly, Ashley only put his neighbours' minds to rest, not their ears! He liked them and felt bad for playing loud music so now he had to <u>reassure</u> them he was determined to change his behaviour.

When you <u>reassure</u> someone, you make their worry go away by making them feel better, or feel relieved. Here you're changing the way they feel about something, not only their beliefs.

ENSURE vs. INSURE

ENSURE

To <u>ensure</u> complete security of his flat, Enzo would lock the door and then try different ways of forcing it open before leaving for work in the morning.

Only then did he hear a little voice in his head say: "Well done Enzo. Now you've really <u>made certain</u> your model train collection is safe".

INSURE

Gerald only learned the real value of his car <u>insurance</u> after he drove into a black limousine with a plate: "<u>Insured</u> by Mafia. You hit us, we hit you."

From then on, when Gerald thought of <u>insurance</u>, he immediately thought of <u>injury</u>.

BORED vs. BOARD

BORED

Mother says she is <u>bored</u> of <u>red</u> dresses, shoes and lipsticks.
Father never gets bored of the <u>red</u> colour on Mother.
He is only <u>bored</u> when waiting at a <u>red</u> light.

"British motorists spend a fifth of their average daily drive
waiting at <u>red</u> lights", he reads off a newspaper.

BOARD

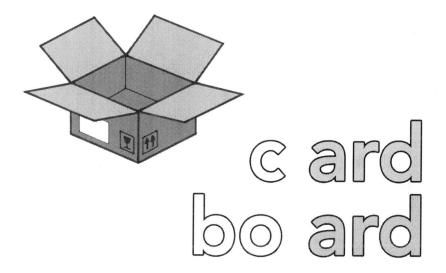

Virtually all <u>cardboard</u> boxes are made of <u>card</u>.
That's the spelling of '<u>board</u>' sorted.

BRAKE vs. BREAK

BRAKE

Bradley had to <u>brake</u> so hard that he scraped asphalt off the road to avoid driving into a <u>bra</u>.

He learned the spelling of the word '<u>brake</u>' for life.

BREAK

Eamonn was a secret ninja. He would <u>break</u> furniture in the office but his boss was never cross – one doesn't cross a ninja!

Luckily, the 'furniture damage' cycle would eventually <u>break</u>, as <u>Ea</u>monn quit his job. Why? He was asked to trace numbers – it's a well-known fact that it's impossible for ninjas to leave a trace.

COFFEE vs. INSTEAD

COFFEE

Don't want to pay a <u>fee</u> for <u>coffee</u>?

INSTEAD

Have a <u>tea</u> ins<u>tea</u>d.

COMMITTEE vs. COMMISSION

COMMITTEE

Who elected Lion as the King of the Jungle? A voting committee made up of two monkeys, two tigers, and two elephants.

They reserved the right to remain anonymous so we can't list their names.

COMMISSION

The election results were verified by a specially formed <u>commission</u> made up of <u>two mo</u>nkeys and <u>two s</u>nakes.

Stephen and Stuart were the snakes.

All votes were declared valid.

COMPLEMENT vs. COMPLIMENT

COMPLEMENT

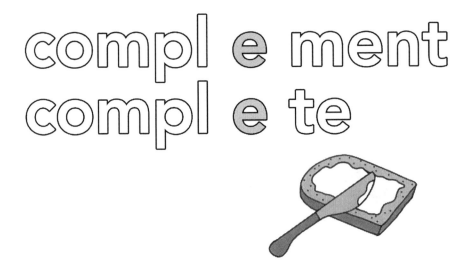

Butter <u>completes</u> bread – the two <u>complement</u> each other.

Other matching pairs are fish and chips, strawberries and cream, cheese and crackers, Sherlock and that doctor... Doctor Who or Dr Watson?

COMPLIMENT

Who doesn't like <u>compliment**s**</u>?

"<u>I</u> like nothing more than a genuine, heart-felt <u>compliment</u>", said Ken while studying himself in a mirror. Barbie's face lit up. She looked up and whispered: "Go on then. <u>I</u>'m ready for the <u>compliment!</u>"

DESERT vs. DESSERT

DESERT

Fewer than a quarter of all known <u>deserts</u> are covered in <u>sand</u>, yet when we hear the word 'desert', we think of <u>sand</u>.

Icy Antarctica is the largest cold desert on Earth. It's bigger than the Sahara with all its <u>sand</u> spreading over 12 countries!

DESSERT

The word 'dessert' comes from the French 'desservir', which means 'to clear the table'.

I know someone who holds an unofficial world record for fastest table clearing when sweet stuff is served!

EMIGRATE vs. IMMIGRATE

EMIGRATE

When you <u>emigrate</u>, you <u>exit</u> (leave) your country to live in another one.

When goods are sold to another country, it's called <u>ex</u>port, as they exit (leave) the country.

IMMIGRATE

When you <u>immigrate</u>, you come <u>into</u> a new country.

When goods are bought from another country, it's called <u>im</u>port, as they come into the country.

FLOUR vs. FLOWER

FLOUR

Mother only uses <u>flour</u> from <u>our</u> local mill because it makes the best bread, cakes and pancakes.

She calls, "Get me four pounds of <u>our flour</u>", and one of us runs to the local mill.

FLOWER

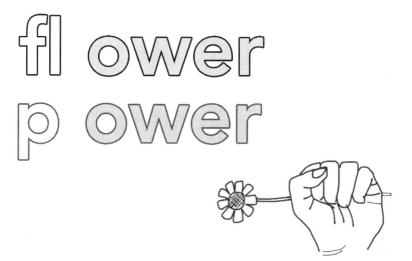

Why do we love flowers? Their beauty feeds our souls. Their colours and smells seduce us so that we give them full attention. That is their secret power – flower power.

I find it a lovely, nostalgic thought that in the 60s and 70s people believed that flower power would make the world a better, safer place.

HAIR vs. HARE

HAIR

I dry my hair in the air.

Unless it's humid out there – I don't want to be Lion King.

HARE

Apparently you <u>are</u> faster than Tortoise, Hare.

<u>ARE</u> you?

HOLE vs. WHOLE

HOLE

Here I am, a tiny hole in the middle of a Polo mint inside a packet for sale (in mint condition, of course).

WHOLE

The tiny Polo <u>hole</u> only exists when the mint is <u>whole</u>.

That's how the little <u>hole</u> has the last laugh:
"You can eat the mint but you can never eat me!"

LOSE vs. LOOSE

LOSE

It's easy to <u>lose</u> track of how fast we <u>lose</u> money because each time we tend to think of it as a <u>single</u> amount:

"I didn't <u>lose</u> one hundred pounds, I spent a <u>single</u> amount that was £100."

LOOSE

Why does Betty have <u>loose</u> teeth?
She thought candy floss and dental floss was the same thing.

But there is something that keeps her <u>loose</u> teeth together.
It's <u>tooth</u>paste.

NECESSARY vs. OCCASIONALLY

NECESSARY

It is <u>necessary</u> for Mother to have coffee with two sugars.
One coffee, two sugars. One C, two Ss.

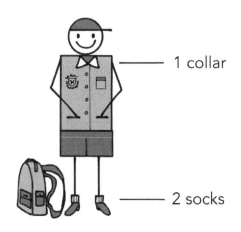

1 collar

2 socks

Father prefers to draw a
schoolboy with one collar
and two socks.
One C, two Ss.

OCCASIONALLY

Occasionally, Mother and her friend go on a diet. She makes two coffees (one for her, one for her friend) with only one spoonful of sugar split between the two cups. Two coffees, one sugar. Two Cs, one S.

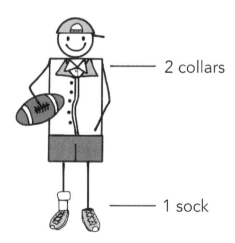

2 collars

1 sock

Father draws a boy – a rugby player – with two collars and one sock. Two Cs, one S.

He explains: "The boy was in a hurry to play rugby and didn't take his school shirt off – he's wearing two collars. He didn't care he'd lost a sock and rushed onto the field to kick the ball."

PEACE vs. PIECE

PEACE

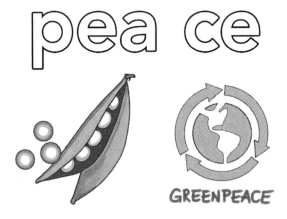

GREENPEACE

A tiny pea is a very peaceful creature. It's so peaceful that Greenpeace used its colour to represent their values.

green pea = green peace = Greenpeace

Really? Hang on a minute. Pete has made it all up. But what a story... Now you remember the spelling of 'peace'.

PIECE

There's nothing else to say other than "Have a piece of pie."

PHYSIOLOGY vs. PSYCHOLOGY

PHYSIOLOGY

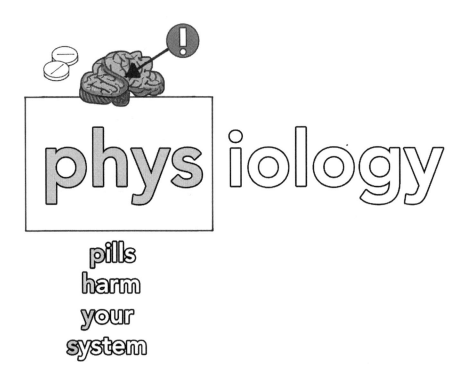

phys iology

pills
harm
your
system

Pills help many people live normal lives, although when someone is addicted to pills, they struggle to function normally without taking them.

Physiology is about normal functioning of living organisms and their systems and parts, such as the brain.

PSYCHOLOGY

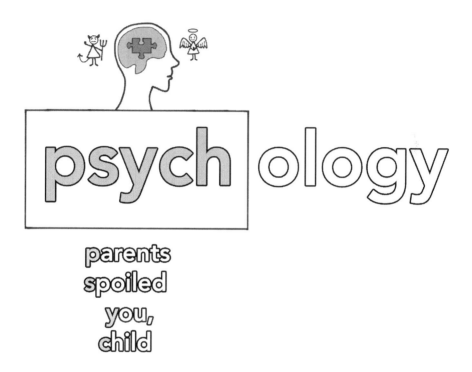

Freud argued that it was your mother who single-handedly 'spoiled you, child'. Modern psychology came to recognise that it's only fair that both parents share the blame.

Both psychology and psychiatry have the same spelling pattern 'psych'. Is there any difference between the two?

Psychiatrists are medically trained, psychologists are not.

PRINCIPAL vs. PRINCIPLE

PRINCIPAL

A fortune cookie told Tommy that the first person he would greet in the morning was his best <u>pal</u> for life.

The Principal was not impressed.
Poor Tommy.
Detention for a month.

PRINCIPLE

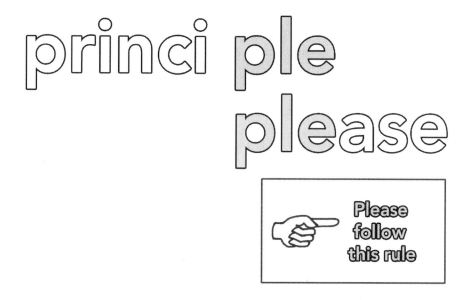

It's always best to follow <u>rules</u> as a matter of <u>principle</u>, but what about rules that have a double-meaning?
Here's one:

SLOW
MEN AT WORK

'<u>Pl</u>ease Slow Down' would do just the trick.

PRONOUNCE vs. PRONUNCIATION

PRONOUNCE

Picture this scene: a United Nations conference at the height of its activities and <u>no UN</u> interpreter can pronounce the code word for 'lunch break'.

A very long conference with very hungry participants indeed...

PRONUNCIATION

Sister Louisa was a most trustworthy and dependable <u>nun</u>.

Once, the <u>CIA</u> tried to make her confess correct <u>pronunciation</u> of secret words.

Worry not. <u>Nun</u>'s the word.

QUIET vs. QUITE

QUIET

Ellie is keeping it <u>quiet</u> that she is on a <u>diet</u>.

She wants to fit into a model size wedding dress but shhh... be <u>quiet</u>, the groom doesn't know either.

QUITE

Bryn only sometimes opens doors for other people. But he always lets his dog pass through first.

Bryn isn't terribly polite. He is only quite polite.

STATIONARY vs. STATIONERY

STATIONARY

Ahoy, Matey. Ye want t'be <u>stationary</u>?

<u>Anchor</u> the ship then, <u>a</u>rrrr.

STATIONERY

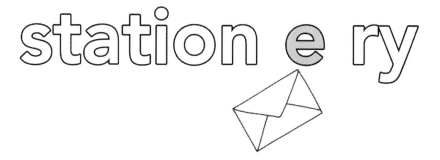

We asked a hundred people to name an item of <u>stationery</u>.

Ninety nine said '<u>envelope</u>'.

TALL vs. TALK

TALL

Taylor stood up on both toes, locked his knees and stretched his <u>legs</u> to be as <u>tall</u> as he could be.

TALK

When Taylor <u>talked</u>, he bent one leg to the side – he didn't know why but it helped others spell the word '<u>talk</u>'.

THAN vs. THEN

THAN

Jack was taller <u>than</u> Dan.

Why did Dan borrow a l<u>a</u>dder before he went to see Jack?
So they could see eye to eye.

THEN

"And <u>then</u> I... I..."
"What DID you do <u>next</u>?"
"<u>Then</u> I apologised".
"Oh, that's settled <u>then</u>".

THEIR vs. THERE vs. THEY'RE

THEIR

Their Irish friends were very jolly.

When they didn't sing, they danced. When they didn't dance, they drank Guinness. And when they drank Guinness, they told side splitting jokes that only their Irish friends could understand.

THERE

"There they are."
"Where?"

Start with HERE. If it's not HERE, it's over THERE.

WHERE?
Over THERE.

THEY'RE

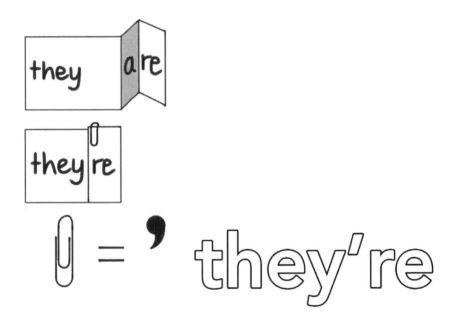

Think paper clip, think apostrophe.

NOTES

TOO vs. TWO

TOO

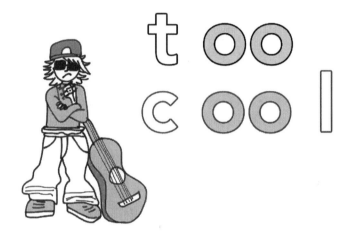

Toon was too cool for a cartoon character.
He was too talented to stay cool on TV.
Toon wrote his own songs and played his own gigs.
Toon was too cool.
Did I mention he was a song writer too?

TWO

There can only be <u>two</u> <u>twins</u>.
One, two.
<u>Two</u> <u>tw</u>irling and <u>twi</u>sting <u>twins</u>.

WEAR vs. WHERE

WEAR

Earrings were originally rings that women fastened to their ear lobes (ear rings). Nowadays, we have all sorts of pierced and non-pierced (clip on) earrings.

WHERE

"There they are."
"Where?"

Start with HERE. If it's not HERE, it's over THERE.

WHERE?
Over THERE.

WEATHER vs. WHETHER

WEATHER

What's the <u>weather</u> at s<u>ea</u> like today?

The <u>weather at sea</u> is not looking great.
A storm is on its way.

WHETHER

He thought long and hard about <u>whether</u> he should do it.

"I don't know <u>whether</u> I should apply for the job, or <u>whether</u> I should stay in college", <u>he</u> said.

<u>He</u> didn't realise it then but only <u>he</u> knew the answer.

WHO'S vs. WHOSE

WHO'S

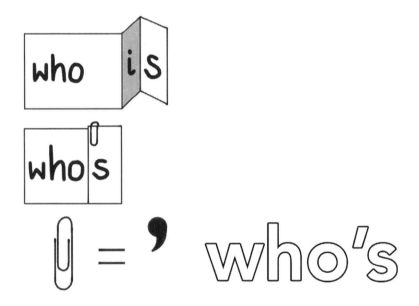

Think paper clip, think apostrophe.

WHOSE

"Whose rose is this?" wondered the little prince.

He thought she was so beautiful he had to look after her until she became strong enough to look after herself.

WITCH vs. WHICH

WITCH

Why do <u>wit</u>ches cackle?
Because they are <u>wit</u>ty.

Or another way:

Why do w<u>itch</u>es ride on broomsticks?
Because they have <u>itch</u>y feet.

WHICH

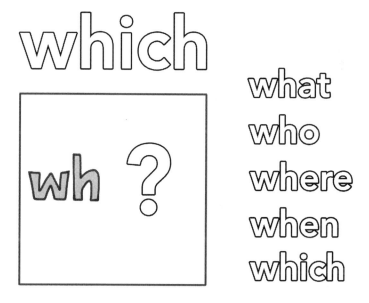

Which is yet another question that starts with 'wh'.

YOUR vs. YOU'RE

YOUR

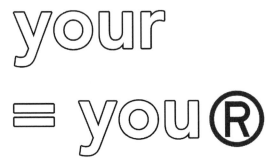

Checklist:
- Does it belong to him, her or them?
- Do they own it?

If you answered YES:
Put the R at the end of YOUR. Just as the trademark sign ®
is placed after a name that is protected because it belongs to
an organisation.

If you answered NO:
It's YOU'RE. No R at the end of the word.

YOU'RE

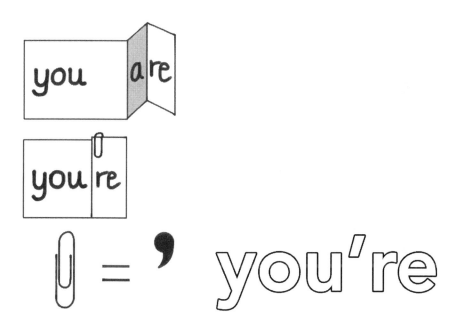

Think paper clip, think apostrophe.

S or C?
ADVISE vs. ADVICE
LICENSE vs. LICENCE
PRACTISE vs. PRACTICE

Meet <u>S</u>nake, an active animal that <u>s</u>lides in a <u>s</u>erpentine motion.

<u>C</u>at, on the other hand, is a <u>comfort creature</u> that lacks any motivation to be active when it doesn't have to be.

These two have important jobs to do when it comes to spelling:

S = verb
doing word

C = noun
non-doing word

When you <u>advise</u> someone, you do it actively by speaking or writing to them. In contrast, a piece of <u>advice</u>, or the <u>advice</u>, is given to you without any effort on your part.

to advise

the advice

You have to physically <u>license</u> your car as opposed to obtaining a <u>licence</u> in the post.

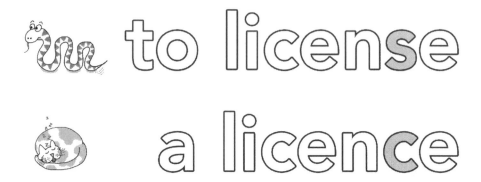

I <u>practise</u> law (it's a lot of hard work but the money is good). My legal <u>practice</u> (the building) is over there.

NOTES

4 TRICKY EVERYDAY WORDS

ACCIDENT

Des had an <u>accident</u>: "The <u>cars collided</u>, somehow, and now there's a <u>dent</u>... in the other car."

ACHIEVE

Adam never suspected <u>Eve</u> would want to <u>achieve</u> the same financial status as him.

It only took her just over a hundred thousand years to <u>achieve</u> that.

Good on you, <u>Eve</u>. What an <u>achieve</u>ment!

ADDRESS

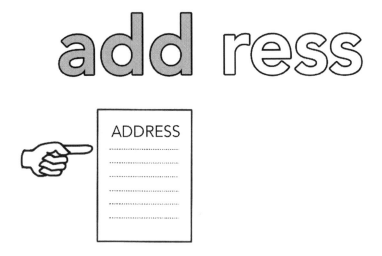

"Add your address here", I was told before I added the address on the form.

ANSWER

"A very good <u>answer</u> will earn you <u>two ticks</u>", promised Miss Pell as she set homework for next week.

ANXIETY

Andy suffers from e<u>x</u>am <u>anxiety</u>. He is <u>anx</u>ious about a big <u>X</u> next to his answer. "<u>An X in exams</u> is the worst that can happen!"

APPEAR

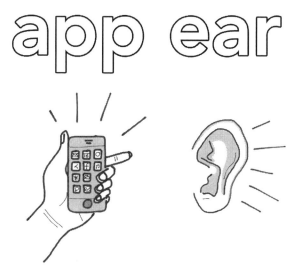

A new <u>app</u> has <u>appeared</u> to test your dominant <u>ear</u>.
You can now hold the phone to the right <u>ear</u>.
Like this Alfie, get it right!

But what about people who hold it to the left <u>ear</u>?

ARCHITECT

Is it true that only an <u>architect</u> can design an <u>arch</u>?
My brother is an engineer.

Both architects and engineers design arches.

Engineers ensure arches withstand strong physical pressure.
Architects make sure that arches are pleasing to look at.

ARGUMENT

Arnie's argument was that he could only think logically when he chewed gum: "No gum, no debate."

We couldn't argue with that.

AWKWARD

That <u>awkward</u> moment when you realise that <u>W</u>aldo <u>k</u>illed <u>W</u>ally.

Wait a minute, say that again: <u>who</u> <u>k</u>illed <u>W</u>ally??

BARGAIN

"A good <u>bargain</u> is always a <u>gain</u>", gasped Barney before he rushed to the next shop.

BEAUTIFUL

be au tiful
be au thentic

"To be <u>beautiful</u> you need to <u>be</u> <u>au</u>thentic" is Bea's life motto.

BEGINNING

In the <u>beginning</u>, the world was created as a mirror image of the creator himself.

BELIEVE

"I want to <u>believe</u> him but what if it's a <u>lie</u>?" thought Bella while packing her suitcase. Liam had told her they were going on a holiday to Narnia.

BISCUIT

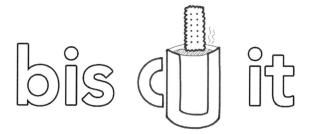

You've tried dipping a <u>biscuit</u> in your tea, now put a <u>cup</u> in your biscuit to spell the word correctly.

BRAIN

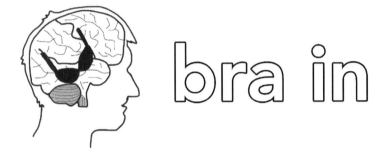

Bradley learned to spell 'brake' after he avoided driving over a bra. The incident is still firmly stuck in his brain.

Brain scans revealed bra images in the areas associated with a strong emotional response. The bra is actually in Bradley's brain!

BRILLIANT

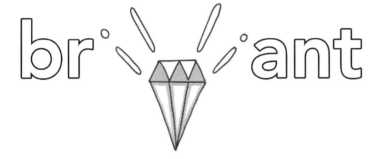

A <u>brilliant</u> is a diamond with symmetrical edges that send sparkling beams of light. <u>Brilliant</u>!

Now put that bri<u>ll</u>iant away. The beams are making me <u>ill</u>.

BROCCOLI

br **occo** li
Mor **occo**

Don't be surprised to find br<u>occo</u>li in traditional dishes of Mor<u>occo</u>. Have you tried spiced quinoa with roasted br<u>occo</u>li and chickpeas?

CALENDAR

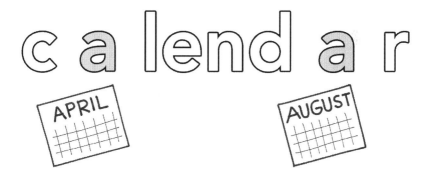

Only two months in the whole year start with an A.
Lend me a calendar so I can check.

CARIBBEAN

Who would have thought that there is a <u>rib</u> and a <u>bean</u> in the dish associated with the <u>Caribbean</u> when spelling the word?

CEMETERY

Every time Celia had to pass through the <u>cemetery</u>, she was heard utter a quiet "<u>Eee</u>k."

DEBT

<u>De</u>nis carried the <u>b</u>urden of his <u>debt</u> with dignity.

DIFFERENT

Be <u>different</u>, <u>e</u>mbrace the change. Don't <u>e</u>liminate the E in the middle of the word. It gives you an <u>e</u>dge. It <u>e</u>mpowers you to do things you've always wanted to do.

<u>E</u>mulate new <u>e</u>nergy to <u>e</u>mphasise your <u>difference</u>.

EMBARRASS

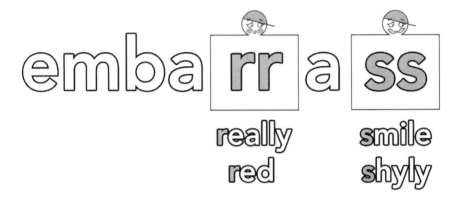

When Rodney is <u>embarrassed</u>, he goes <u>r</u>eally <u>r</u>ed and <u>s</u>miles <u>s</u>hyly.

Some people say Rodney is an <u>ass</u>.

ENGINEER

Don't you sn<u>eer</u> at an <u>engineer</u>. They are hard-headed people, you know.

EQUIPMENT

When I said, "Get your <u>equipment</u> ready", I didn't mean your telephones.

There is <u>no letter t</u> in equipment, is there?

EXAGGERATE

My <u>ex</u>-boyfriend was a <u>gentle giant</u>. People used to
<u>exaggerate</u> that he was as big as a great grizzly bear.
To me, he was as small as a grain of gold.
The only gigantic thing about my <u>gentle giant</u> was his heart.

EXCELLENT

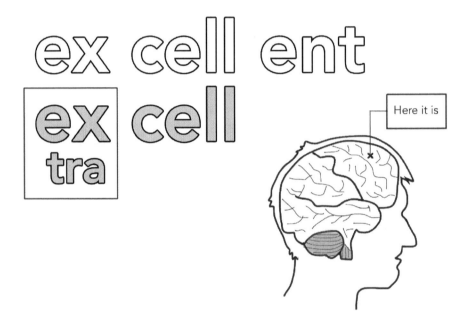

Why are some people <u>excellent</u> problem solvers?

They must have an <u>extra cell</u> in their brains. How else would they come up with <u>excellent</u> ideas like a three-day weekend?

FAMILIAR

fami liar

"How can someone so <u>familiar</u> be such a <u>liar</u>?" thought Florence looking at Fiona's boyfriend's nose. It seemed improbable that Fiona was not <u>familiar</u> with the wooden puppet story.

"Liar, liar, pants on fire. Nose as long as a telephone wire", sang Florence as she left the room.

FEBRUARY

There is only one month in the whole year that makes me go "Brrr…"

February is impossibly cold in this part of Britain.

FOREIGN

<u>E</u>uro is a <u>foreign</u> currency.

The spelling of the word looks like it belongs to a '<u>foreign</u>' language.

FORTUNATE

for tuna te

Why is Pebbles the most <u>fortunate</u> cat in the world?
He gets to eat lots of <u>tuna</u>.

Just check my tuna-exclusive cupboard. It's <u>for tuna</u> only.

FRIEND

Freddie wasn't simply a <u>Fri</u>day friend.

He was a <u>friend</u> till the <u>end</u>!

GARAGE

What's this <u>rage</u> in the <u>garage</u>?

Sue bought a new car this morning.
It doesn't fit in the <u>garage</u>.

HICCUP

To cure a <u>hiccup</u>, try drinking tea from a <u>cup</u> while standing on your head.

HOMEOWNER

ho meow ner

Yes, 'homeowner' is one word, I promise.

The cute sound effect in the middle of the word will help you remember who the real homeowner is! Meow...

HONOUR

We promise <u>on</u> <u>our</u> <u>h</u>onour!

IRRESISTIBLE

My <u>sister</u> and <u>I</u> are simply <u>irresistible</u>.

By the way, I don't see any table in '<u>irresistible</u>', do you?

ISLAND

Island is land.

If I could only take one thing to the desert island...
I wouldn't go.

ISSUE

Why is Sue the issue every time?

Possibly because she doesn't realise she is the issue every time.

JEALOUSY

"Not many things in life make you feel as <u>lousy</u> as <u>jealousy</u>", admitted <u>Jean</u>'s ex-boyfriend.

LEATHER

I eat her

"This <u>leather</u> handbag is so nice I could <u>eat her</u>!" thought Lena while deciding whether to spend her last £20 on lunch or accessories.

LEISURE

"Let's eat ice-cream."
"Sure".

LIBRARY

Following his <u>bra</u>king incident to avoid driving over a <u>bra</u>, which left emotional and physical scars on his <u>bra</u>in, Bradley decided to find self-help books in the li<u>bra</u>ry.

Little did he know that he would see another <u>bra</u> in the li<u>bra</u>ry.

MESSAGE

A Facebook <u>message</u>:

"My house isn't <u>messy</u>. It's custom designed by my 3-year-old. We live in a new <u>mess age</u>, which gives children freedom to learn by exploring."

Like or comment?

MONEY

Tell your friends (individually) they'll owe you <u>one</u> penny if you can read their mind. Here's your script:

1. Pick a number between 1 and 10.
2. Multiply it by 9.
3. If you've got a 2-digit number, add the two digits together.
4. Take away 5.
5. Give your digit a letter: 1 = A, 2 = B, 3 = C, etc.
6. Think of a country that begins with that letter.
7. Now find the second letter in the country and think of an animal that begins with that letter.
8. Think of that animal's colour.
9. Is it a grey elephant from Denmark?
10. Can I have <u>one</u> penny please?

PAVILION

There might be very many lions in a <u>million</u>, but there is only one <u>lion</u> in a <u>pavilion</u>.

One <u>lion</u>, one <u>L</u>.

PEOPLE

<u>People</u> live on the Earth and the round planet (<u>O</u>) lives in the spelling of the word '<u>people</u>'.

POSSESSES

'Possesses' possesses five Ss.

But what about
'possession', or
'possessive'?

Four out of five is still impressive.

QUEUE

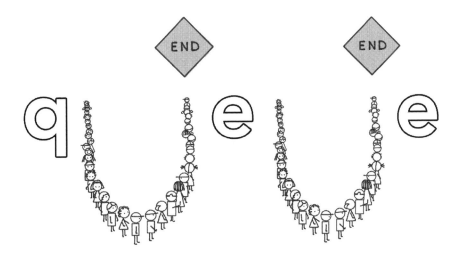

Line up in a semi-circle until you see the 'End' sign.
Repeat and you have the spelling of '<u>queue</u>'.

RASPBERRY

"Pick me", shouted the raspberry.

Save distressed <u>raspberries</u> from acting <u>p</u>eculiar – <u>pick</u> them!

RECEIVE

When you smile, you <u>receive</u> a smile back.

Public transport and corridors are great places to test this theory, but please don't stare, or smile for longer than a couple of seconds.

Let me know how many smiles you <u>rece</u>ived back.

RECOVER

When my illness is <u>over</u>, I <u>recover</u>.

Will I <u>recover</u> what I paid (<u>over</u> the odds) for the holiday that made me ill? I should think so.

RESTAURANT

"Ey, you! Get out of my restaurant!" heard Reggie after he'd tasted food on nearby tables.

Not the wisest way to choose your dinner.

SAUSAGE

Although <u>sausages</u> originated in Germany, the <u>USA</u> gave us hotdogs and corndogs.

Mustard or ketchup with yours?

SCISSORS

"<u>Cut it or else!</u>", hissed a bold customer to his barber who'd dropped <u>scissors</u>.

"Absolutely, sir. I was just about to ask about your holidays", mumbled the barber, as he made a parting in the customer's imaginary hair.

SPECIAL

Spencer was a <u>special</u> agent with the <u>CIA</u>.
He wore <u>special</u> glasses from spe<u>cia</u>list opti<u>cia</u>ns.

SURFACE

On the <u>surface</u>, Steve looked like an average guy. One day, he felt a strong urge to be the best.

Fast forward to today, Steve isn't just an <u>ace</u>, he is a <u>surf ace</u>!

TOGETHER

"To be <u>together</u>, I need <u>to get her</u>!" shouted <u>Toby</u>.

Too late – <u>Her</u>mione disappeared round the corner.

TOMORROW

Tim could see Tom or go rowing <u>tomorrow</u>:

"<u>Tom or row</u>? Well, if the weather is good, I'll go rowing. If it's not good, I'll go rowing anyway."

TOUCH

I told Tom that when I <u>touch</u> my neck, I can't help but scream "<u>Ouch</u>!" I had pulled a muscle.

Tom told me his story: "When we took Grandad to a restaurant, we realised he's like a computer. We had to <u>touch</u> him every few minutes or he would fall asleep. "<u>Ouch</u>! What?" "It's okay Grandad. Thanks for letting me have your dessert."

Tom laughed but I wasn't <u>touched</u> by the story. I ate his snack to teach him a lesson. It was peanut butter and cucumber. <u>Ouch</u>!

VICIOUS

Committing crime is a <u>vice</u> of <u>vic</u>ious people.

VILLAGE

Not all <u>villages</u> have a <u>villa</u> in them but those that do help us spell the word '<u>village</u>'.

WATCH

Watch out for the letter *t* in watch.

Not *t* for Timex but the silent *t* in the middle of the word 'watch'.

WEDNESDAY

"Payday is my favourite day."
"If I had a favourite day, it'd be <u>Wed-Nes-day</u>."
"You haven't even met <u>Nes</u>."
"I said, IF I had a favourite day... I'd marry <u>Nes</u> any <u>day</u>."
"Even on a <u>Wednesday</u>?"

WEIRD

There is nothing strange, creepy, or freaky about <u>weird</u> creatures.

They are 100% a<u>we</u>some.

WRAP

"Wrap it well or it will come undone", warned Wilma at the exact time as Will's ham, lettuce, tomatoes, mushrooms, sweet corn and sweet mustard sauce landed on her new wall-to-wall carpet.

5 TRICKY FORMAL/ACADEMIC WORDS

ACCOMMODATE

<u>Accommodate</u> is such a long word that it can <u>accommodate</u> not one but <u>two Cs</u> and <u>two Ms</u>. Now, that's <u>accommodating</u>.

Oooh, a very nice window in your <u>accommodation</u>.

AMIABLE

"<u>Am</u> <u>I</u> <u>able</u> to help you, Sir?"
"Oh, you're very <u>amiable</u>, Sir."

APPARENT

Apparently, there is an app for parents to control the amount of time kids spend on their electronic devices.

Unfortunately, the app requires the kids' help with apparent installation problems.

ASCERTAIN

When you <u>ascertain</u> (check) the facts, it makes you <u>as certain</u> as you can be.

ASSASSINATE

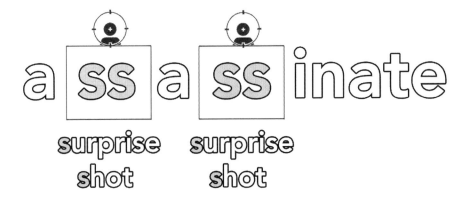

<u>A</u> surprise <u>s</u>hot, then <u>a</u>nother <u>s</u>urprise <u>s</u>hot.

The target has been <u>assassinated</u>.

ATHEIST

An <u>atheist</u> might want to disprove the existence of God or gods using <u>the</u>ory-based evidence.

BUSINESS

If it weren't for the good old <u>bus</u> <u>in</u> <u>Ess</u>ex, how would busy <u>business</u>men from the region get to their <u>business</u> meetings in London?

What's that, Buster? No good bu<u>sin</u>ess is free of <u>sin</u>?

CAPABILITY

Carter was especially <u>able</u> when he put his thinking <u>cap</u> on.

His outstanding <u>capability</u> was reported in local papers, which labelled him the '<u>cap-able</u> boy'.

CHALLENGE

If it won't <u>challenge</u> you, it won't <u>change</u> you.
<u>L</u>ong-<u>l</u>asting <u>e</u>ffect guaranteed!

COMMITMENT

Mick expressed his <u>commitment</u> to Mary with two words: "<u>M</u>arry <u>me</u>!"

DEFINITE

I didn't know I'd be so lucky but I was <u>definitely</u> <u>in it</u> to win it! This is the only <u>definite</u> answer I can give, <u>in it</u>?

DILEMMA

Emma has a dilemma.
She gave her porcelain doll to Gemma,
who dropped it when she felt a tremor.
Gemma has now confided in Jemma,
who thinks Emma should condemn her.
Is that how Emma should solve the dilemma?

DISCIPLINE

I <u>disc</u>ipline my dog by only letting him play with his <u>disc</u> when he's been good. It's '<u>disc-ipline</u>'.

ENVIRONMENT

Iron is in our environment. Remember to put 'iron' in the spelling too.

By recycling scrap iron, we save up to 75% of the energy needed to make products from raw materials. That makes for a happy environment!

FLUORESCENT

Felix's eyes turned <u>fluorescent</u>.
Was it because of his <u>flu, or E scent</u>s in the flu pills?

It's hard to tell but E numbers and flavoured scents are best avoided.

FORESEEABLE

Florence can <u>foresee</u> future events. You <u>see</u>, she is <u>able</u> to know what will happen in the near future.

Words that start with '<u>fore</u>' mean things that are at the <u>front</u> or close to us, for example '<u>foreseeable</u>' means 'in the <u>near</u> <u>future</u>'.

GIST

When you <u>get</u> the <u>gist</u> of something, you have a broad understanding of what has happened, or the text's key points.

Mind mapping is a great way to <u>get</u> the <u>gist</u>. <u>Get it</u>?

GLOSSARY

Without a <u>glossary</u>, I'm at a <u>loss</u>.

GOVERNMENT

A Politics exam question:

"The <u>government</u> has <u>no</u> <u>money</u> of its own. It's all your money. Discuss."

GRAFFITI

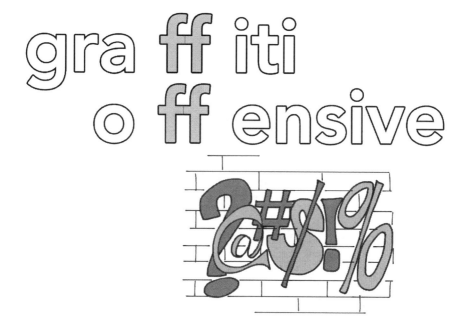

"Offensive or not, graffiti is a form of art."
"Yes, but don't forget that graffiti is illegal."

"You're still here? Put those spray cans back in your bag. Don't hang around. Off you go!"

GRAMMAR

Poor <u>grammar</u> doesn't reflect well on you.

What's that? The reflection in the mirror needs fixing? Why is '<u>grammar</u>' always tricky?

HERITAGE

Can we put a price <u>tag</u> on something as priceless as the national and world <u>heritage</u>?

HIERARCHY

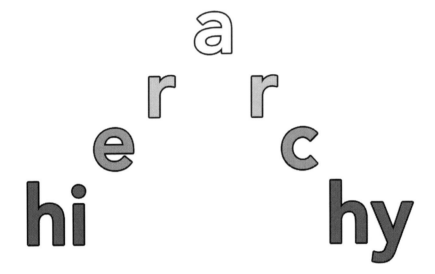

Father showed me an uncanny mirror image chart that represents the order of social standing. Everyone seems to be above me!

Here's what it said:

<u>A</u>-list entries
<u>R</u>ank entries
<u>E</u>arn-your-<u>C</u>orn entries
and you: <u>Hi</u> there! Hy!

IMMEDIATELY

You need to do this <u>immediately</u>.
<u>Act</u> now!

INDEPENDENT

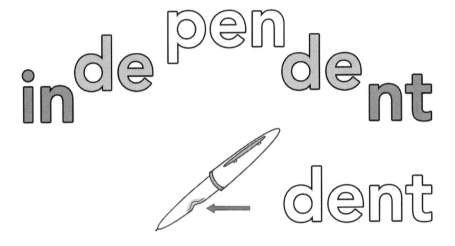

How do you tell if a journalist is <u>independent</u>?
By a <u>dent</u> in their <u>pen</u>.

Another way to spell the word right is to picture two DEs around 'pen'.

KNOWLEDGE

kn owl edge

Apparently, the <u>owl</u> has the most kn<u>owl</u>edge of all birds. No wonder the owl has the <u>edge</u>!

When I spell '<u>knowledge</u>', I see an <u>owl</u> sitting on the <u>edge</u> of a branch. Or I imagine the same <u>owl</u> feeling on <u>edge</u>!

LIAISON

<u>Liaison</u> involves communicating with someone.

There was only one thing Tarzan wanted to communicate to Lia, his mother: "<u>Lia, I son</u>".

MANAGEMENT

Is your management a gem? A shining example of an excellent company?

MANOEUVRE

man oeu vre

**old
elephants
usually**

<u>O</u>ld <u>e</u>lephants <u>u</u>sually man<u>oeu</u>vre badly.

Or, as Father suggested, "<u>Man o EU v</u>oted <u>red</u>".

MEDIEVAL

me die val

People would <u>die</u> early in <u>Medieval</u> times. If it wasn't the Black Death, it was famine, violence or heresy.

If you know a handful of heretics in modern-day politics and media, you could say that old habits <u>die</u> hard.

MISSPELL

Miss Pell was a stickler for correct spelling.

"Miss Pell, I would never misspell a word to upset you", said Peter, self-proclaimed greatest fan of Miss Pell.

NOTICEABLE

notice able

before

after

"I hope you're <u>able</u> to <u>notice</u> the difference between the two boards. I worked really hard to make sure it's <u>noticeable</u>."

(>_<)

"Oh… You *have* noticed…"

OCCURRED

A déjà vu is when we have a feeling that our current experience has <u>occurred</u> before.

There are twice the number of Cs and Rs in the spelling of 'occurred' – now check that each letter has <u>occurred</u> twice.

OPPORTUNITY

When an <u>opportunity</u> knocks on your door, give <u>two knocks</u> back for a yes.

"If only Father knew that," sighs Mother. "He knocks three times and wonders why nobody answers."

PARALLEL

Not many things are as <u>parallel</u> as train tracks.

The tracks in the spelling litera<u>ll</u>y show the meaning of <u>parallel</u>.

PARLIAMENT

How do you become a <u>parliament</u>? You 'forget' to summon it, as Charles I did in the 17th century.
For 11 years, he WAS the parl<u>iam</u>ent!

Ah, I almost forgot – that didn't work out very well.
He was later beheaded for treason...

PERSISTENT

per sis tent

No one is more <u>persistent</u> than my <u>sister</u>. She should hold the world record for taking the slowest time to put up a <u>tent</u>.

"To be <u>persistent</u> is to refuse to quit", says my <u>sis</u>. "Anyway, if I stopped trying to put up the <u>tent</u>, where would I sleep tonight?"

PHARAOH

My history teacher joked that Ancient Egypt wouldn't have fallen to the Roman Empire if the pharaohs had succeeded in teaching their aras to repeat the emperors' secret conversations.

"Oh" was the most they achieved.

PHYSICIAN

It's easy to confuse <u>physicians</u> with physicists. Phy<u>sic</u>ians treat <u>sick</u> people, and physicists research physics.

Take <u>Ian</u>. He became a phy<u>sician</u> to heal the <u>sick</u>.

PREJUDICE

"It's silly to be horrible to someone just because they have different colour spots", concluded 4-year-old <u>Judi</u> after her mother used <u>dice</u> to explain the word '<u>prejudice</u>'.

PRIVILEGE

A broken <u>leg</u>? It's your <u>privilege</u> to use a special seat.

PROFESSOR

| One F | one face | check √ |
| Two Ss | two specs | check √ |

What is the professor still looking for?

PROPAGANDA

Is Halloween a <u>pro-pagan</u> celebration?

Prunella seems to think so: "The only thing we learn from Halloween is that pretending to be someone else, not working hard and living a good life, results in a sweet reward."

PUBLICLY

To be truly effective when speaking <u>publicly</u>, you need to <u>love yourself</u>. Thanks, Justin.

If you thought public speaking was your ally, think again – there is no -ally at the end of the word. Only <u>-ly</u>, <u>love yourself</u>.

RECOMMEND

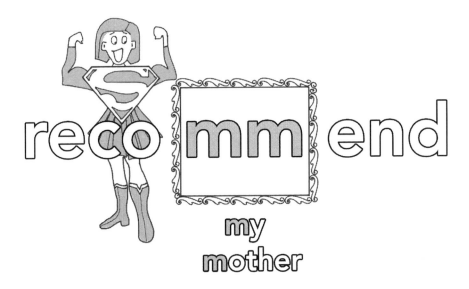

Any job anywhere: big, small, in house, out of house, skilled, semi-skilled, tough, dirty, unsociable hours – I <u>recommend</u> <u>m</u>y <u>m</u>other!

RESEARCH

When I think of <u>research</u>, I first imagine a <u>sea</u> of papers. Books, articles, print-outs, slides, notes, sticky notes – a dangerous, cold and unforgiving <u>sea</u>.

But if you tread carefully, the same <u>sea</u> can be awe aspiring, breathtaking, mesmerising and actually rather beautiful.

SCHEDULE

sch ool
sch edule

Bus schedule, mail delivery schedule, work schedule, house chore schedule?

Think 'school schedule' to remember the spelling of any schedule.

SEPARATE

Separate the sheep from the goats and remember to leave <u>a rat</u> in '<u>separate</u>'.

SIGNIFICANT

"Please sign here, Sir."
"What if I can't?"
"Then we've got a significant problem, Sir. No signature, no loan."

SUCCESS

If, at first, <u>success</u> avoids you, you and I have a lot in common.
Unless your road to <u>success</u> is always under construction, in which case I suggest you deactivate your Facebook and Instagram accounts.

THESAURUS

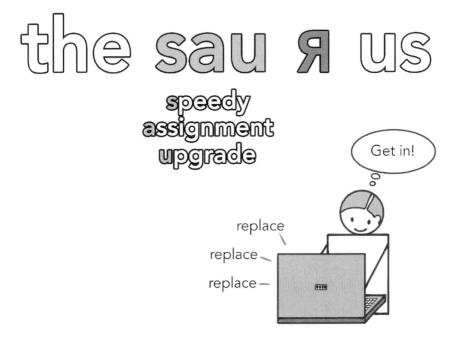

Ted has made friends with a <u>thesaurus</u>: "I feel like I'm in a toy shop! So many words to choose from. A <u>s</u>peedy <u>a</u>ssignment <u>u</u>pgrade every time. Get in!"

VACUUM

A Philosophy exam question:

"How soon do you become a <u>vacuum cleaner</u> when you clean a <u>vacuum cleaner</u>?"

VILLAIN

"Villa in live you?" asked Yoda.
"I do, do I?" answered the villain.
"Live not on evil," replied Yoda in the villain's speaking style.

6 UNFORTUNATE WORDS WITHIN WORDS

Here's a handful of amusing, terrifying or 'simply wrong' – as Mother has put it – unfortunate words within words, which can hold extra memorable spelling hints!

DYSFUNCTIONAL

dys fun ctional

Join in the fun, or... run?

EXECUTE

exe cute

Can anyone be too <u>cute</u>? Never!

Unless they are about to exe<u>cute</u> or electro<u>cute</u>...

GHOST

g host

When you asked for the <u>host</u> to take you round the house, you didn't think it would be a <u>ghost</u>, did you?

PHARMACY

Dispensing pills or ills?

RESOURCE

re sour ce

Some meetings to discuss <u>resources</u> are more 'sour' than others.

SLAUGHTER

Stop <u>laugh</u>ing and put the chicken down, you <u>s</u>avage!

THEATRE

When she said it'd be a <u>heat</u>ed evening at the <u>theatre</u>, I didn't think she meant this kind of <u>heat</u>!

TODDLER

There's nothing <u>odd</u> about a t<u>odd</u>ler.

tod-dler (noun) – emotionally unstable, pint-sized dictator with the uncanny ability to know exactly how far to push you towards utter insanity before reverting to a lovable cuddle-monster.

7 REFERENCES

CARTOONS

In accordance with the copyright law, to the extent of 'fair dealing', small fragments (references to characters only) from well-known works and visuals have been used in some cartoons (drawn by hand by the author) for the purpose of humourous effect (parody) to maximise learning outcomes by means of powerful memory associations with well-known visual material.

Films: *Finding Nemo, Tarzan, Star Wars*

TV programmes: *The Simpsons*

Literary works: *The Little Prince, Find Wally, Find Waldo*

Games: *Pac-Man*

Logos: *American Atheists, CIA, English Heritage, Greenpeace, Lotto, Toys-R-Us, United Nations*

Intellectual Property Office (2014) *Exceptions to Copyright: Guidance for Creators and Copyright Owners.* October 2014. Newport: IPO. Pp. 5-6.

MNEMONICS

Many mnemonics used in this book are in the public domain – they are widely used by teachers, parents and grandparents. They are shared and handed down from one generation to another. Stylistic variations exist but the underlying ideas have remained unchanged for years. For this reason, it's virtually impossible to trace the exact origin of a particular mnemonic.

Around half of the spelling hints in this book have been collected over the past twelve years when the author worked as a dyslexia support tutor, study skills tutor and psychology teacher. Very many enthusiastic students have shared their favourite mnemonics with me.

The other half are spelling hints created by the author and her students, in particular university teacher training students preparing for their QTS spelling tests. These mnemonics had to pass their tough test of effectiveness before appearing in this book.

INDIVIDUAL MNEMONICS

ADOPT
Broadwell, L. (2016) *8 Things You Should Know About Adoption.* Parents (online). Available at:
http://www.parents.com/parenting/adoption/101/8-things-you-should-know-about-adoption

ARCHITECT
Margolius, I. (2008) *Architects + Engineers = Structures.* Cambridge, Massachusetts: Academic Press.

BORED
Huntingford, S. (2016) Revealed: how long you really spend waiting at traffic lights. *The Telegraph.* Lifestyle: Cars. 15 April 2016.

BREAK
McDonald, A. (2015) *36 Jokes About Ninjas, Because We Love You And We Also Love Ninjas.* Huffpost Comedy (online). Available at:
http://www.huffingtonpost.com/entry/ninja-jokes_us_55e887f2e4b0aec9f3568550

DESERT
Parker, S. (2009) *Deserts (Planet Earth).* London: QED Publishing.

DESSERT
Durand, M. (2013) *French Words, Phrases and Sentences 1000+.* US: Create Space Independent Publishing Platform.

ENVIRONMENT
Business Recycling (2016) *Why Recycle?* (online). Available at: http://businessrecycling.com.au/recycle/iron-steel

FLOWER
Thompson, I. (2013) *Summer of '67: Flower Power, Race Riots, Vietnam and the Greatest Soccer Final Played on American Soil.* US: Create Space Independent Publishing Platform.

GOVERNMENT
Aitken, J. (2013) *Margaret Thatcher: Power and Personality.* London: Bloomsbury Continuum Publishing.

ISLAND
The Telegraph (2015) *Darren Walsh wins the award for best joke at Edinburgh Fringe.* 25 August 2015.

LOSE
Cooper, B.B. (2013) *8 Subconscious Mistakes Our Brains Make Every Day – And How to Avoid Them.* Fast Company (online). Available at: http://www.fastcompany.com/3019903/work-smart/8-subconscious-mistakes-our-brains-make-every-day-and-how-to-avoid-them

MONEY
FC (2016) *Grey Elephant in Denmark*. Finance in the Classroom Educational Resources (downloads). Available at: http://financeintheclassroom.org

PARLIAMENT
Scarboro, D. (2005) *England 1625-1660: Charles I, The Civil War and Cromwell* (SHP Advanced History Core Texts). London: Hodder Education.

THEIR
O'Brien, C. (2016) *The Little Book of Irish Jokes*. Chichester: Summersdale Publishers.

TODDLER
The Baby Concierge (2016) *En route* (online). Available at: https://tobabyconcierge.com/2016/03/03/en-route

WEAR
Sherrow, V. (2001) *For Appearance' Sake: The Historical Encyclopedia of Good Looks, Beauty, and Grooming*. Portsmouth: Greenwood Publishing Group.

8 INDEX

Made in the USA
San Bernardino, CA
19 November 2019